Mom's
New Little Instruction Book

The Wise and Witty World of Motherhood

Annie Pigeon

P

PINNACLE BOOKS

PINNACLE BOOKS are published by

Kensington Publishing Corp.
850 Third Avenue
New York, NY 10022
http://www.pinnaclebooks.com

Copyright © 1995 by Annie Pigeon

Pinnacle and the P logo Reg. U.S. Pat. & TM Off.

First Pinnacle Printing: May, 1995
10 9 8 7 6 5 4 3

ISBN: 0-7860-0140-2

Printed in the United States of America

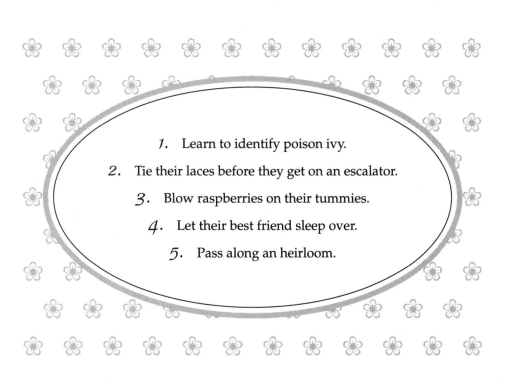

1. Learn to identify poison ivy.

2. Tie their laces before they get on an escalator.

3. Blow raspberries on their tummies.

4. Let their best friend sleep over.

5. Pass along an heirloom.

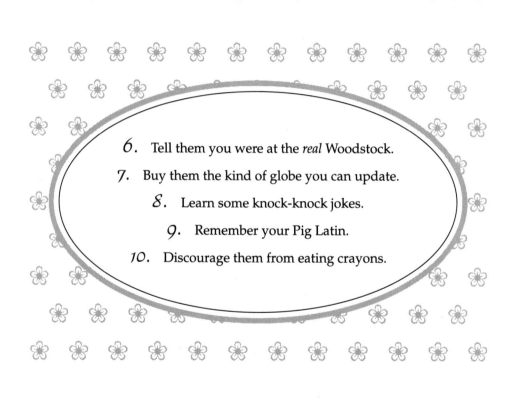

6. Tell them you were at the *real* Woodstock.

7. Buy them the kind of globe you can update.

8. Learn some knock-knock jokes.

9. Remember your Pig Latin.

10. Discourage them from eating crayons.

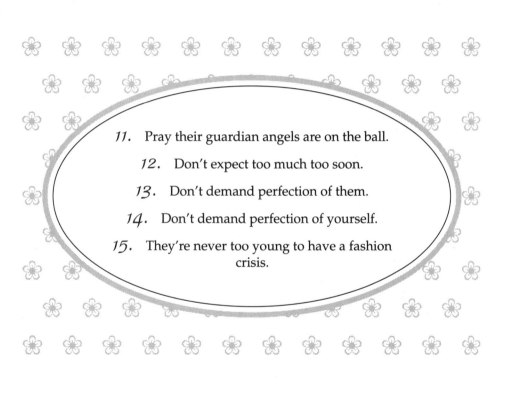

11. Pray their guardian angels are on the ball.

12. Don't expect too much too soon.

13. Don't demand perfection of them.

14. Don't demand perfection of yourself.

15. They're never too young to have a fashion crisis.

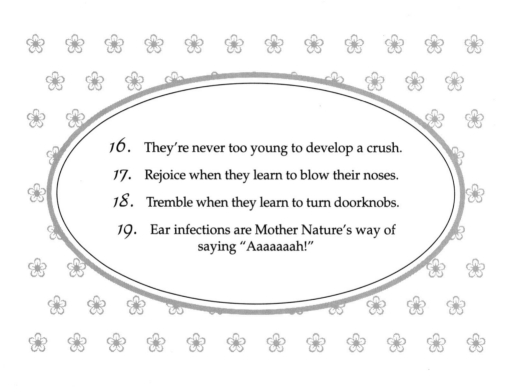

16. They're never too young to develop a crush.

17. Rejoice when they learn to blow their noses.

18. Tremble when they learn to turn doorknobs.

19. Ear infections are Mother Nature's way of saying "Aaaaaaah!"

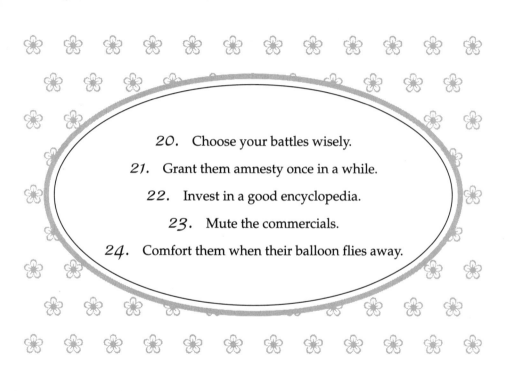

20. Choose your battles wisely.

21. Grant them amnesty once in a while.

22. Invest in a good encyclopedia.

23. Mute the commercials.

24. Comfort them when their balloon flies away.

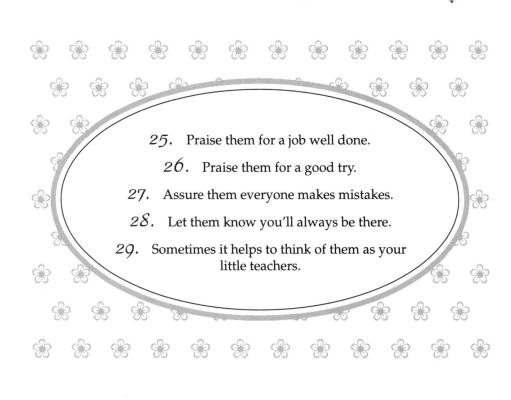

25. Praise them for a job well done.

26. Praise them for a good try.

27. Assure them everyone makes mistakes.

28. Let them know you'll always be there.

29. Sometimes it helps to think of them as your little teachers.

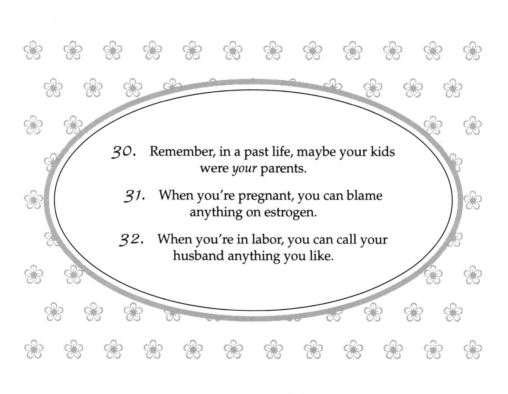

30. Remember, in a past life, maybe your kids were *your* parents.

31. When you're pregnant, you can blame anything on estrogen.

32. When you're in labor, you can call your husband anything you like.

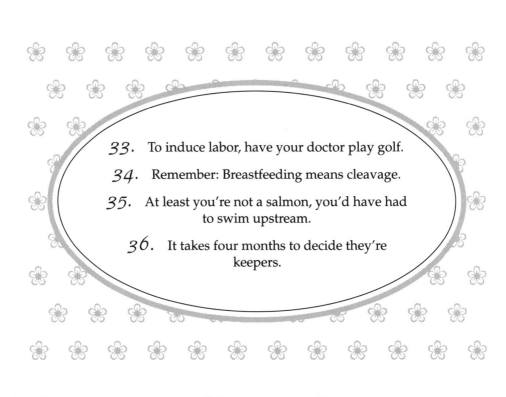

33. To induce labor, have your doctor play golf.

34. Remember: Breastfeeding means cleavage.

35. At least you're not a salmon, you'd have had to swim upstream.

36. It takes four months to decide they're keepers.

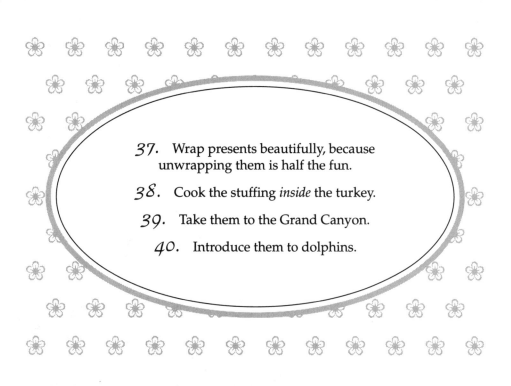

37. Wrap presents beautifully, because unwrapping them is half the fun.

38. Cook the stuffing *inside* the turkey.

39. Take them to the Grand Canyon.

40. Introduce them to dolphins.

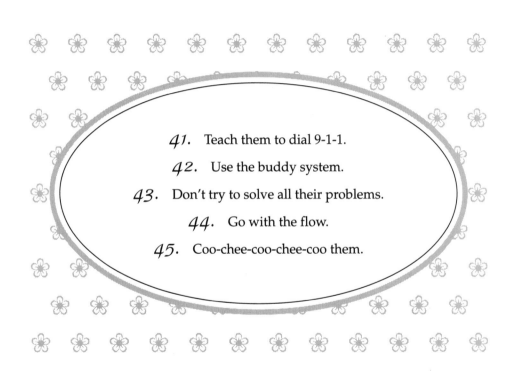

41. Teach them to dial 9-1-1.

42. Use the buddy system.

43. Don't try to solve all their problems.

44. Go with the flow.

45. Coo-chee-coo-chee-coo them.

46. Your toddler's bite means "I love you."

47. Your teen's bite means he's a werewolf.

48. Read only child care experts who have children.

49. Read only child care experts who have a sense of humor.

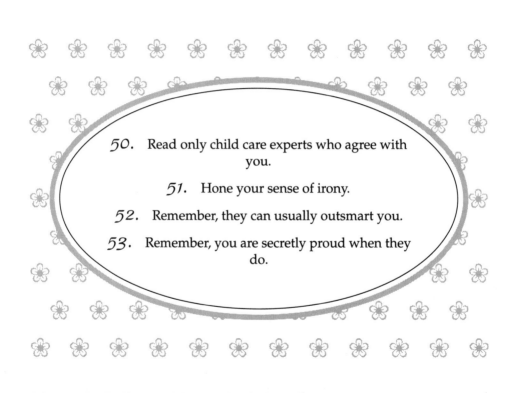

50. Read only child care experts who agree with you.

51. Hone your sense of irony.

52. Remember, they can usually outsmart you.

53. Remember, you are secretly proud when they do.

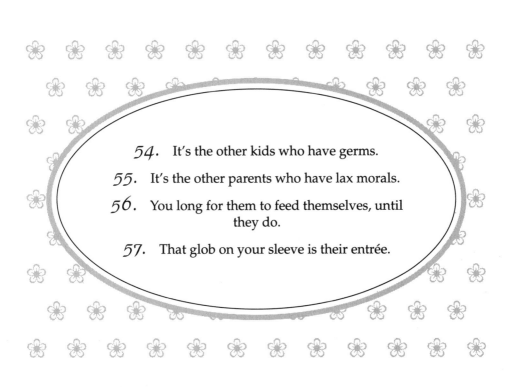

54. It's the other kids who have germs.

55. It's the other parents who have lax morals.

56. You long for them to feed themselves, until they do.

57. That glob on your sleeve is their entrée.

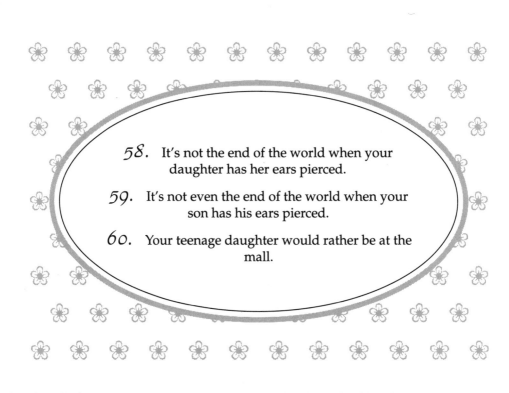

58. It's not the end of the world when your daughter has her ears pierced.

59. It's not even the end of the world when your son has his ears pierced.

60. Your teenage daughter would rather be at the mall.

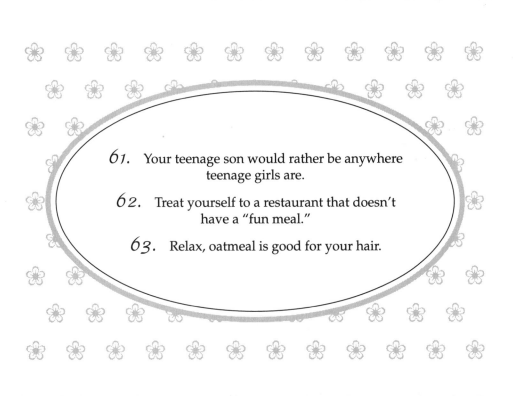

61. Your teenage son would rather be anywhere teenage girls are.

62. Treat yourself to a restaurant that doesn't have a "fun meal."

63. Relax, oatmeal is good for your hair.

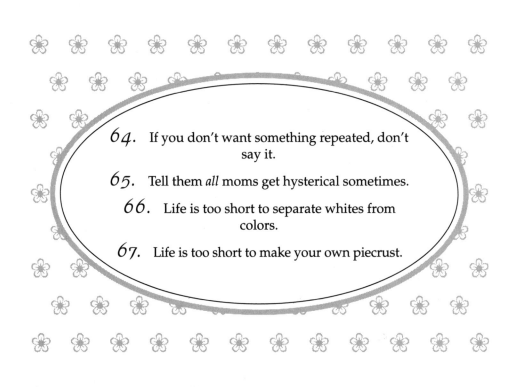

64. If you don't want something repeated, don't say it.

65. Tell them *all* moms get hysterical sometimes.

66. Life is too short to separate whites from colors.

67. Life is too short to make your own piecrust.

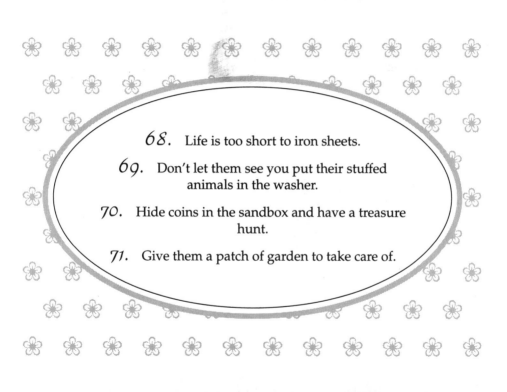

68. Life is too short to iron sheets.

69. Don't let them see you put their stuffed animals in the washer.

70. Hide coins in the sandbox and have a treasure hunt.

71. Give them a patch of garden to take care of.

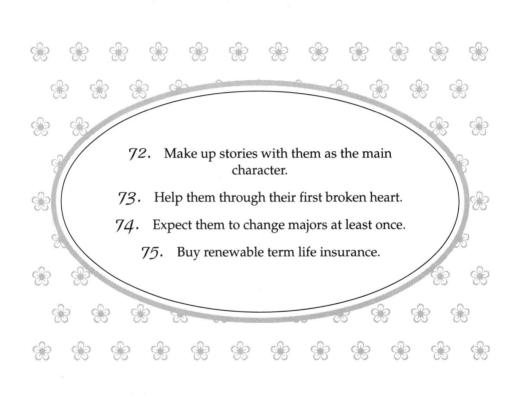

72. Make up stories with them as the main character.

73. Help them through their first broken heart.

74. Expect them to change majors at least once.

75. Buy renewable term life insurance.

76. Save stale bread so they can feed the ducks.

77. Let them run under the lawn sprinkler.

78. Scouting is cool again.

79. Dry cleaners love your toddler.

80. Encourage a daughter who wants to take wood shop.

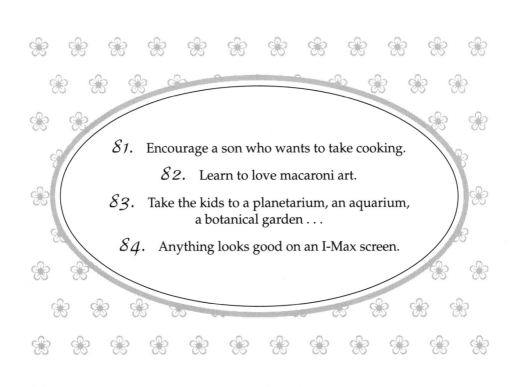

81. Encourage a son who wants to take cooking.

82. Learn to love macaroni art.

83. Take the kids to a planetarium, an aquarium, a botanical garden . . .

84. Anything looks good on an I-Max screen.

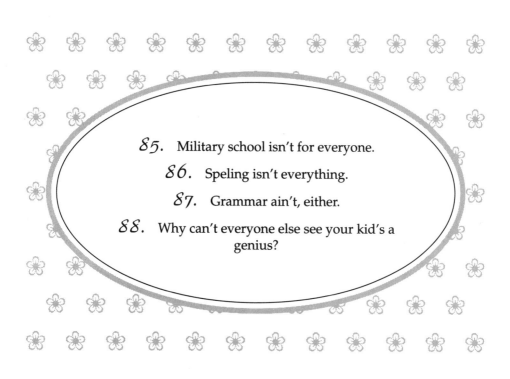

85. Military school isn't for everyone.

86. Speling isn't everything.

87. Grammar ain't, either.

88. Why can't everyone else see your kid's a genius?

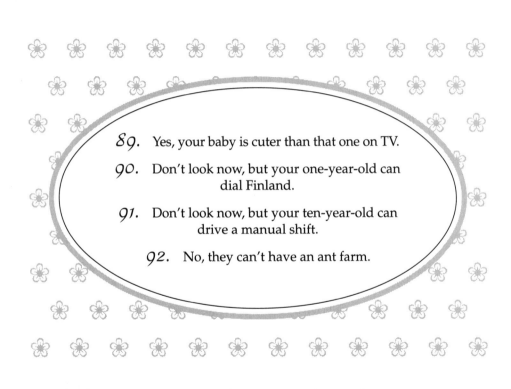

89. Yes, your baby is cuter than that one on TV.

90. Don't look now, but your one-year-old can dial Finland.

91. Don't look now, but your ten-year-old can drive a manual shift.

92. No, they can't have an ant farm.

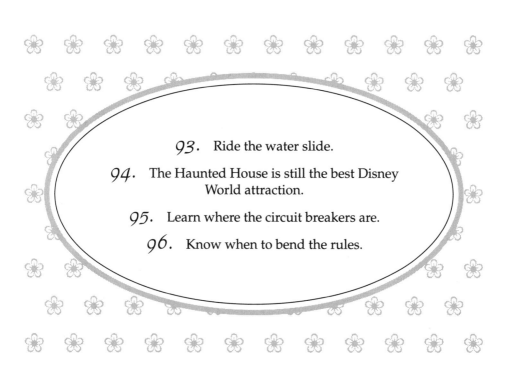

93. Ride the water slide.

94. The Haunted House is still the best Disney World attraction.

95. Learn where the circuit breakers are.

96. Know when to bend the rules.

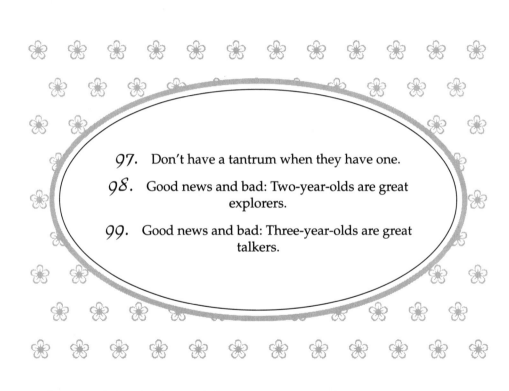

97. Don't have a tantrum when they have one.

98. Good news and bad: Two-year-olds are great explorers.

99. Good news and bad: Three-year-olds are great talkers.

100. Good news and bad: Four-year-olds are great finger-painters.

101. Don't put toast points in your son's lunchbox.

102. Jump in the leaves with them.

103. Learn to make a good pot of chili.

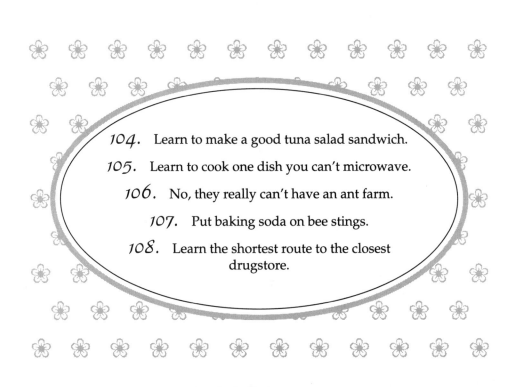

104. Learn to make a good tuna salad sandwich.

105. Learn to cook one dish you can't microwave.

106. No, they really can't have an ant farm.

107. Put baking soda on bee stings.

108. Learn the shortest route to the closest drugstore.

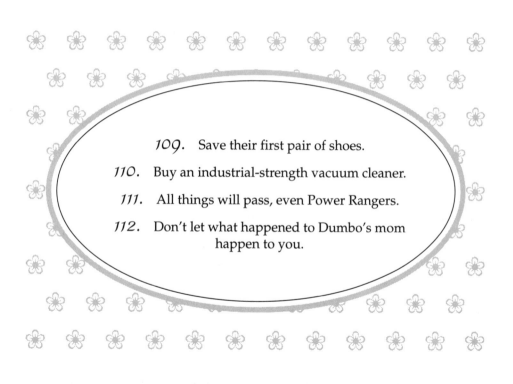

109. Save their first pair of shoes.

110. Buy an industrial-strength vacuum cleaner.

111. All things will pass, even Power Rangers.

112. Don't let what happened to Dumbo's mom happen to you.

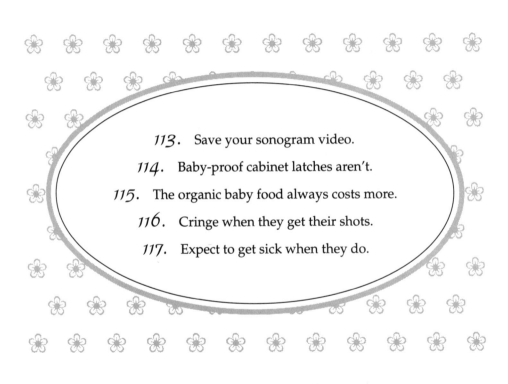

113. Save your sonogram video.

114. Baby-proof cabinet latches aren't.

115. The organic baby food always costs more.

116. Cringe when they get their shots.

117. Expect to get sick when they do.

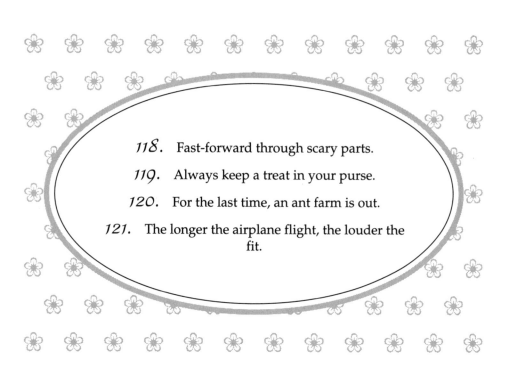

118. Fast-forward through scary parts.

119. Always keep a treat in your purse.

120. For the last time, an ant farm is out.

121. The longer the airplane flight, the louder the fit.

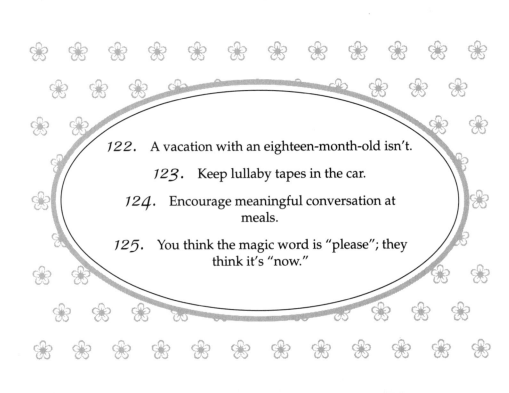

122. A vacation with an eighteen-month-old isn't.

123. Keep lullaby tapes in the car.

124. Encourage meaningful conversation at meals.

125. You think the magic word is "please"; they think it's "now."

126. Accept your limitations.

127. Make the most of your talents.

128. Join in with their play fantasies.

129. If you can't do it while they're napping, you can't do it at all.

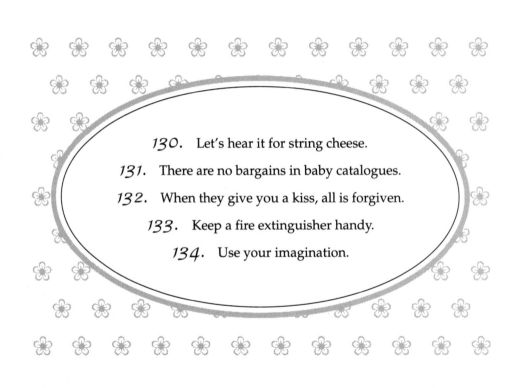

130. Let's hear it for string cheese.

131. There are no bargains in baby catalogues.

132. When they give you a kiss, all is forgiven.

133. Keep a fire extinguisher handy.

134. Use your imagination.

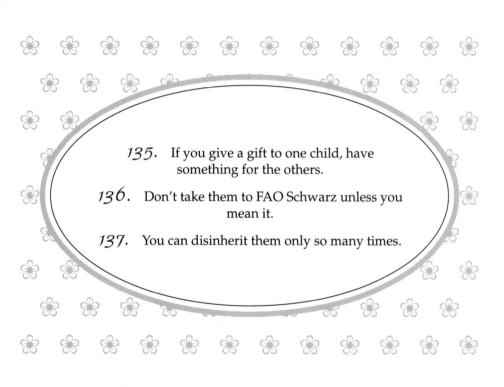

135. If you give a gift to one child, have something for the others.

136. Don't take them to FAO Schwarz unless you mean it.

137. You can disinherit them only so many times.

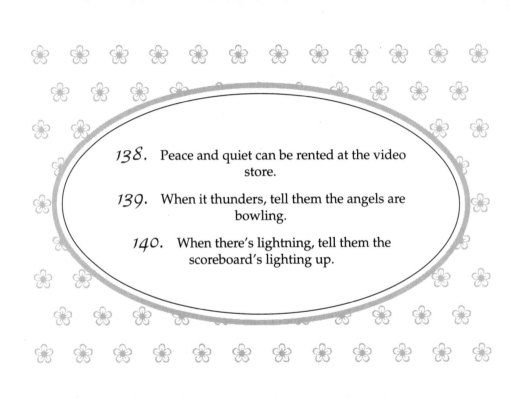

138. Peace and quiet can be rented at the video store.

139. When it thunders, tell them the angels are bowling.

140. When there's lightning, tell them the scoreboard's lighting up.

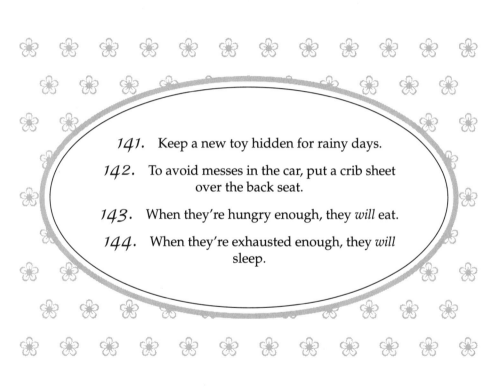

141. Keep a new toy hidden for rainy days.

142. To avoid messes in the car, put a crib sheet over the back seat.

143. When they're hungry enough, they *will* eat.

144. When they're exhausted enough, they *will* sleep.

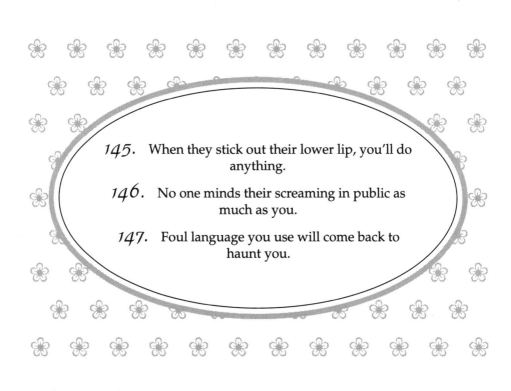

145. When they stick out their lower lip, you'll do anything.

146. No one minds their screaming in public as much as you.

147. Foul language you use will come back to haunt you.

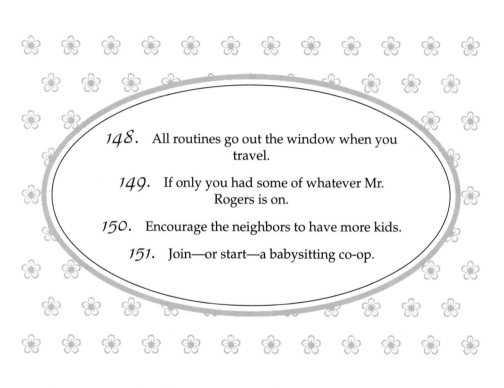

148. All routines go out the window when you travel.

149. If only you had some of whatever Mr. Rogers is on.

150. Encourage the neighbors to have more kids.

151. Join—or start—a babysitting co-op.

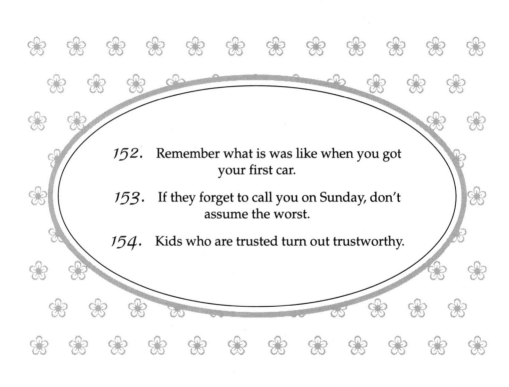

152. Remember what is was like when you got your first car.

153. If they forget to call you on Sunday, don't assume the worst.

154. Kids who are trusted turn out trustworthy.

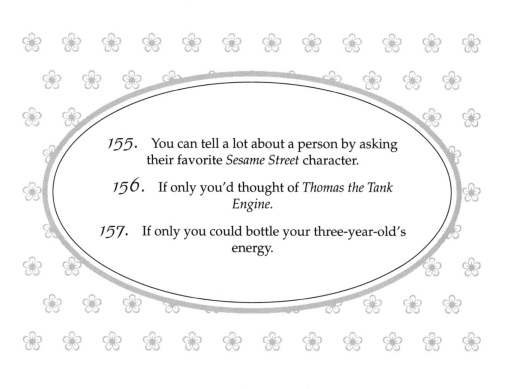

155. You can tell a lot about a person by asking their favorite *Sesame Street* character.

156. If only you'd thought of *Thomas the Tank Engine*.

157. If only you could bottle your three-year-old's energy.

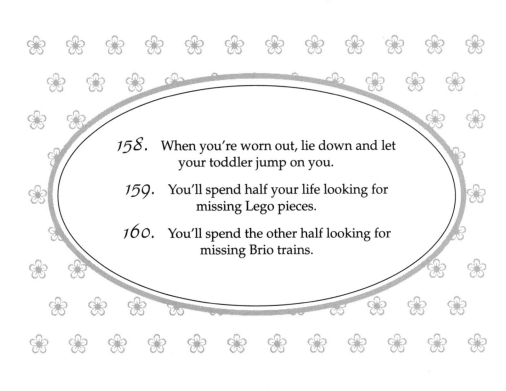

158. When you're worn out, lie down and let your toddler jump on you.

159. You'll spend half your life looking for missing Lego pieces.

160. You'll spend the other half looking for missing Brio trains.

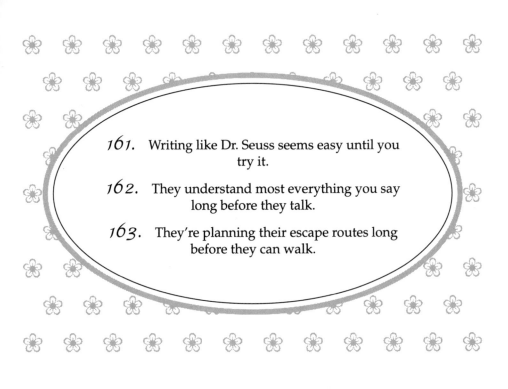

161. Writing like Dr. Seuss seems easy until you try it.

162. They understand most everything you say long before they talk.

163. They're planning their escape routes long before they can walk.

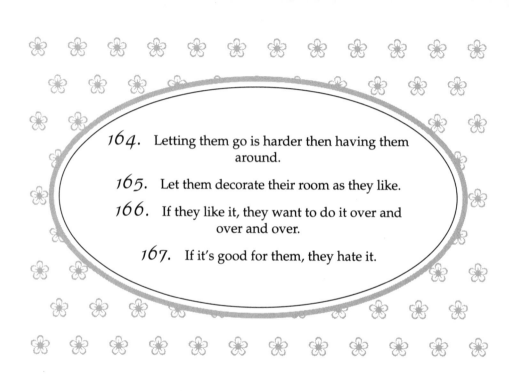

164. Letting them go is harder then having them around.

165. Let them decorate their room as they like.

166. If they like it, they want to do it over and over and over.

167. If it's good for them, they hate it.

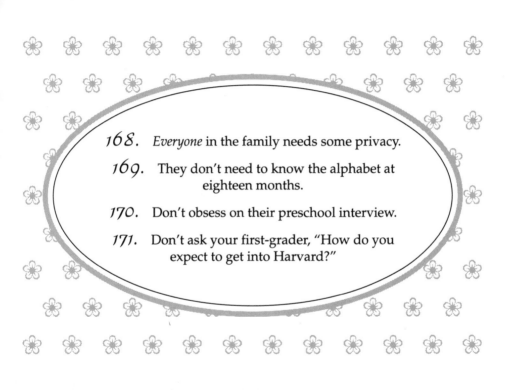

168. *Everyone* in the family needs some privacy.

169. They don't need to know the alphabet at eighteen months.

170. Don't obsess on their preschool interview.

171. Don't ask your first-grader, "How do you expect to get into Harvard?"

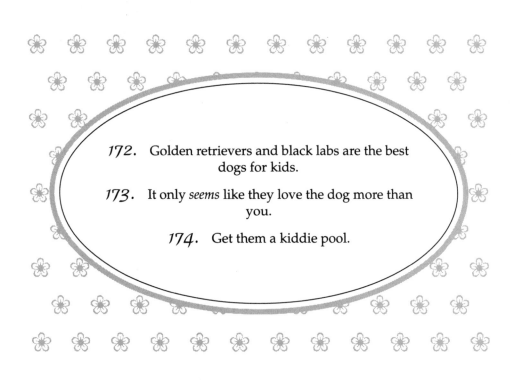

172. Golden retrievers and black labs are the best dogs for kids.

173. It only *seems* like they love the dog more than you.

174. Get them a kiddie pool.

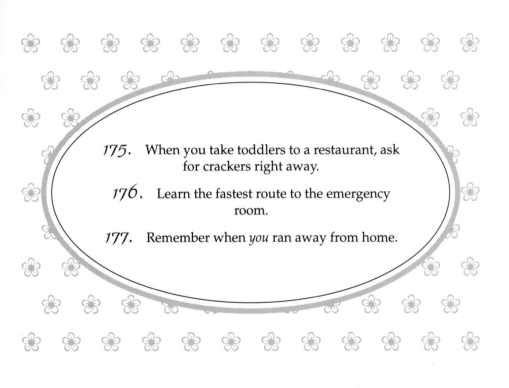

175. When you take toddlers to a restaurant, ask for crackers right away.

176. Learn the fastest route to the emergency room.

177. Remember when *you* ran away from home.

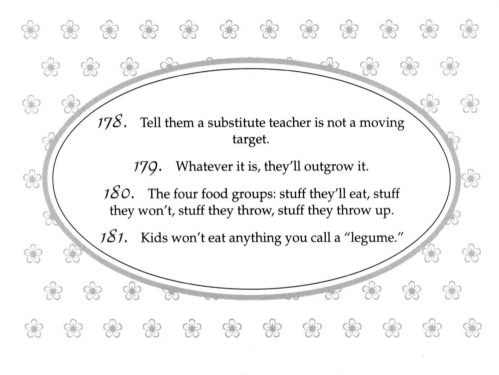

178. Tell them a substitute teacher is not a moving target.

179. Whatever it is, they'll outgrow it.

180. The four food groups: stuff they'll eat, stuff they won't, stuff they throw, stuff they throw up.

181. Kids won't eat anything you call a "legume."

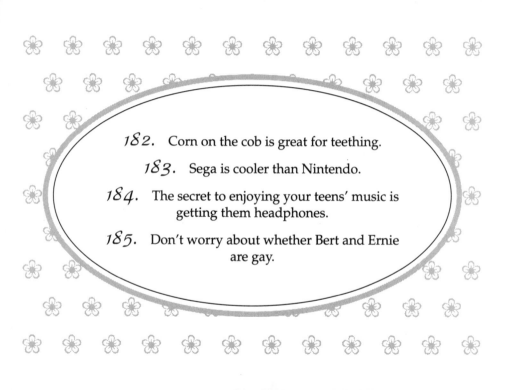

182. Corn on the cob is great for teething.

183. Sega is cooler than Nintendo.

184. The secret to enjoying your teens' music is getting them headphones.

185. Don't worry about whether Bert and Ernie are gay.

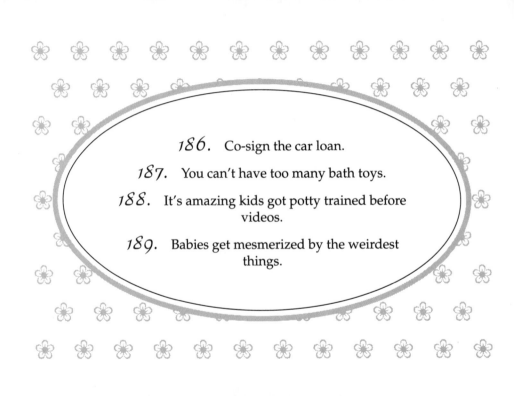

186. Co-sign the car loan.

187. You can't have too many bath toys.

188. It's amazing kids got potty trained before videos.

189. Babies get mesmerized by the weirdest things.

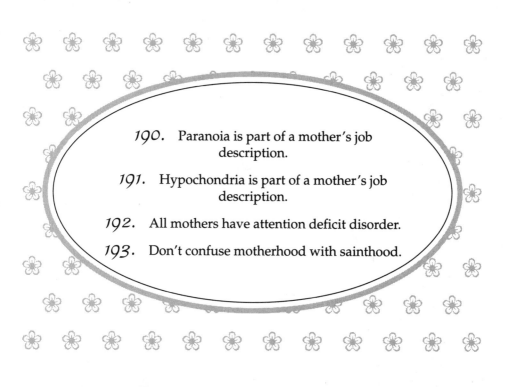

190. Paranoia is part of a mother's job description.

191. Hypochondria is part of a mother's job description.

192. All mothers have attention deficit disorder.

193. Don't confuse motherhood with sainthood.

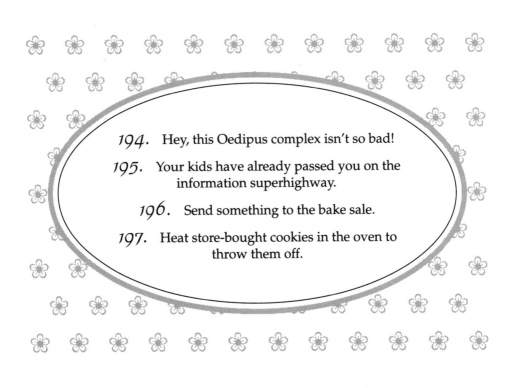

194. Hey, this Oedipus complex isn't so bad!

195. Your kids have already passed you on the information superhighway.

196. Send something to the bake sale.

197. Heat store-bought cookies in the oven to throw them off.

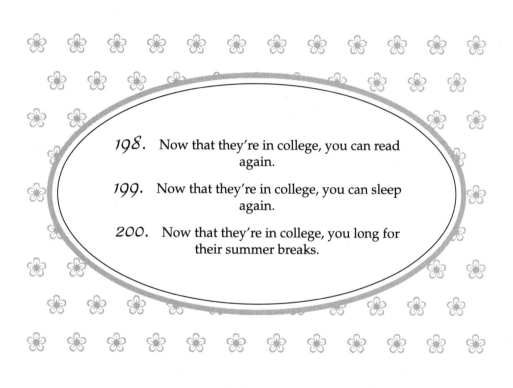

198. Now that they're in college, you can read again.

199. Now that they're in college, you can sleep again.

200. Now that they're in college, you long for their summer breaks.

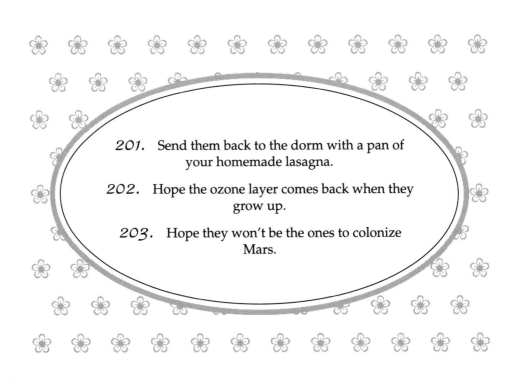

201. Send them back to the dorm with a pan of your homemade lasagna.

202. Hope the ozone layer comes back when they grow up.

203. Hope they won't be the ones to colonize Mars.

204. If they do go to Mars, remind them to take their sweaters.

205. Explain the Golden Rule.

206. Teach by example.

207. Tell them about the new, cheaper ways to call collect.

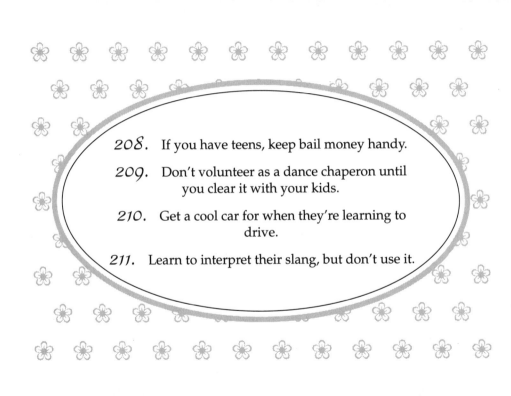

208. If you have teens, keep bail money handy.

209. Don't volunteer as a dance chaperon until you clear it with your kids.

210. Get a cool car for when they're learning to drive.

211. Learn to interpret their slang, but don't use it.

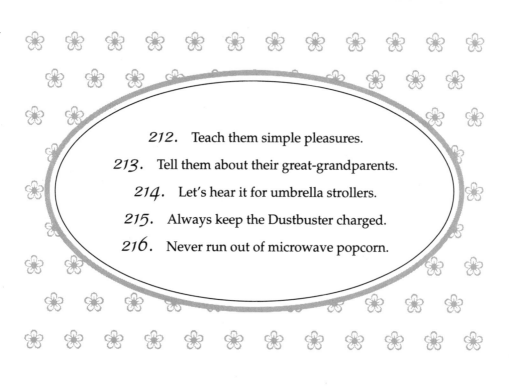

212. Teach them simple pleasures.

213. Tell them about their great-grandparents.

214. Let's hear it for umbrella strollers.

215. Always keep the Dustbuster charged.

216. Never run out of microwave popcorn.

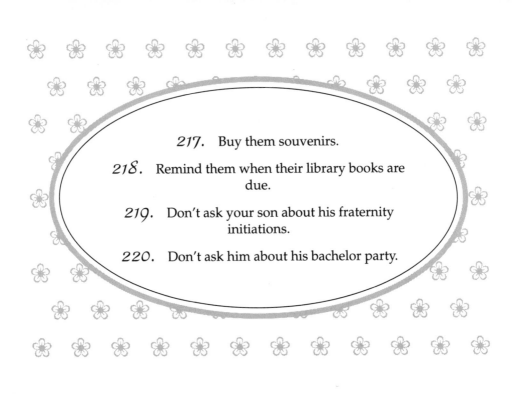

217. Buy them souvenirs.

218. Remind them when their library books are due.

219. Don't ask your son about his fraternity initiations.

220. Don't ask him about his bachelor party.

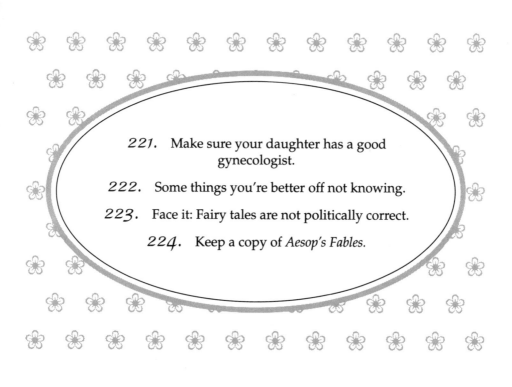

221. Make sure your daughter has a good gynecologist.

222. Some things you're better off not knowing.

223. Face it: Fairy tales are not politically correct.

224. Keep a copy of *Aesop's Fables*.

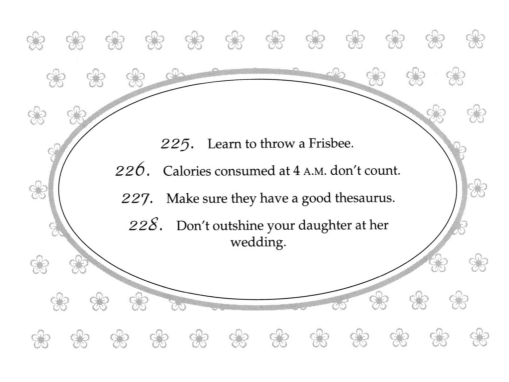

225. Learn to throw a Frisbee.

226. Calories consumed at 4 A.M. don't count.

227. Make sure they have a good thesaurus.

228. Don't outshine your daughter at her wedding.

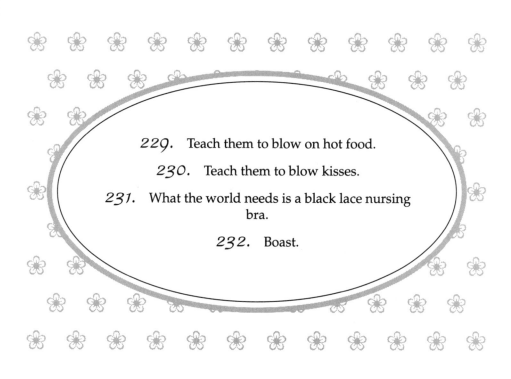

229. Teach them to blow on hot food.

230. Teach them to blow kisses.

231. What the world needs is a black lace nursing bra.

232. Boast.

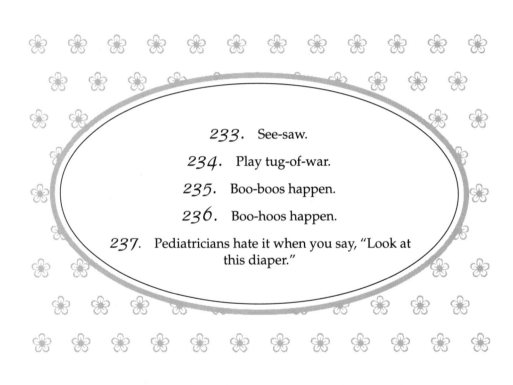

233. See-saw.

234. Play tug-of-war.

235. Boo-boos happen.

236. Boo-hoos happen.

237. Pediatricians hate it when you say, "Look at this diaper."

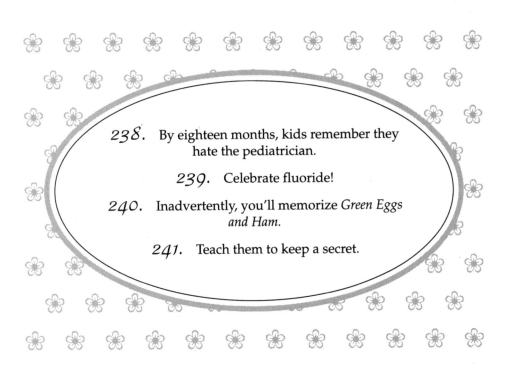

238. By eighteen months, kids remember they hate the pediatrician.

239. Celebrate fluoride!

240. Inadvertently, you'll memorize *Green Eggs and Ham.*

241. Teach them to keep a secret.

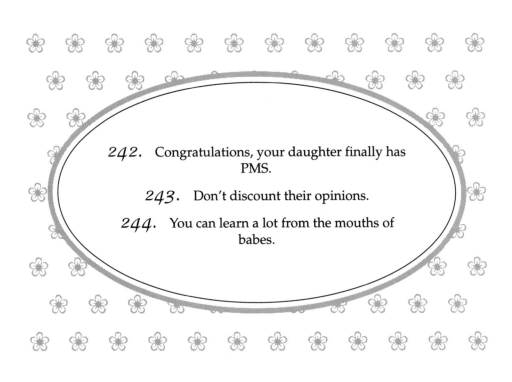

242. Congratulations, your daughter finally has PMS.

243. Don't discount their opinions.

244. You can learn a lot from the mouths of babes.

245. "Because I'm your mother" is a perfectly good reason.

246. Whenever they sprain something, Dad's at the office.

247. Whenever they break something, Dad's out of town.

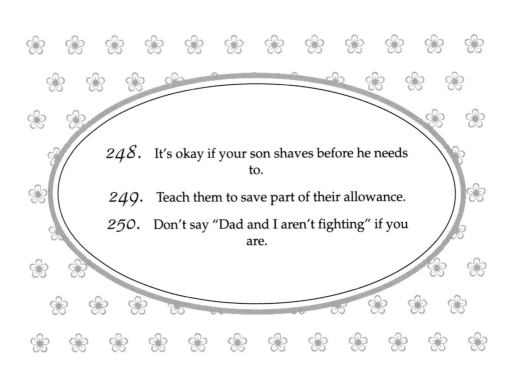

248. It's okay if your son shaves before he needs to.

249. Teach them to save part of their allowance.

250. Don't say "Dad and I aren't fighting" if you are.

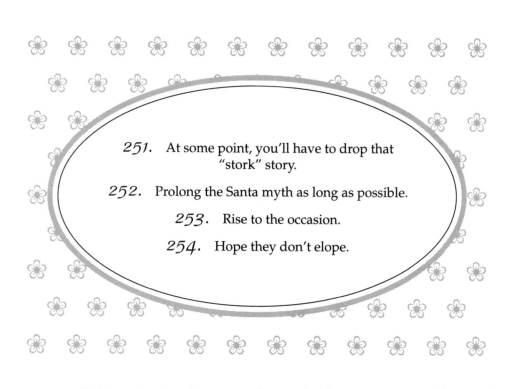

251. At some point, you'll have to drop that "stork" story.

252. Prolong the Santa myth as long as possible.

253. Rise to the occasion.

254. Hope they don't elope.

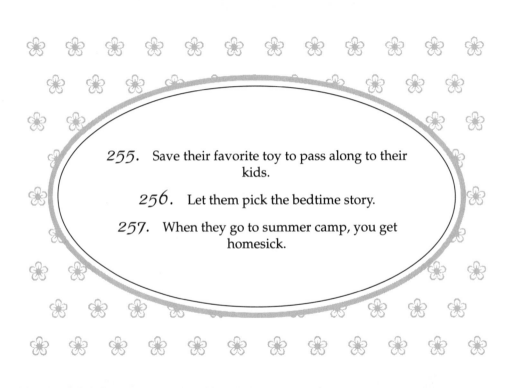

255. Save their favorite toy to pass along to their kids.

256. Let them pick the bedtime story.

257. When they go to summer camp, you get homesick.

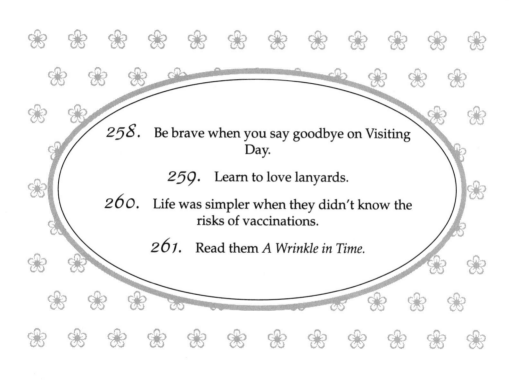

258. Be brave when you say goodbye on Visiting Day.

259. Learn to love lanyards.

260. Life was simpler when they didn't know the risks of vaccinations.

261. Read them *A Wrinkle in Time.*

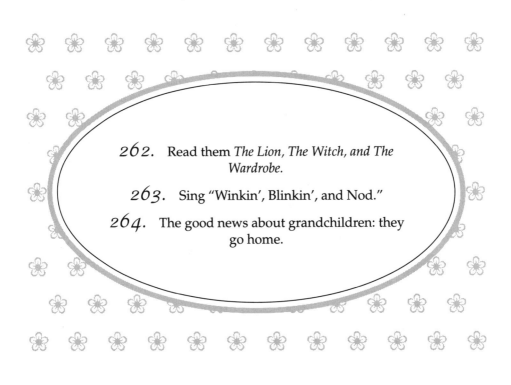

262. Read them *The Lion, The Witch, and The Wardrobe.*

263. Sing "Winkin', Blinkin', and Nod."

264. The good news about grandchildren: they go home.

265. The bad news about grandchildren: they go home.

266. No, you don't *have* to support them while they do a postdoctoral thesis.

267. Okay, they can live at home while they study for the bar.

268. No, they can't live at home when they're a
Supreme Court judge.

269. When your nest is empty, get a Winnebago.

270. They don't want to know if you and Dad
still have a love life.

271. No, you can't go along on their honeymoon.

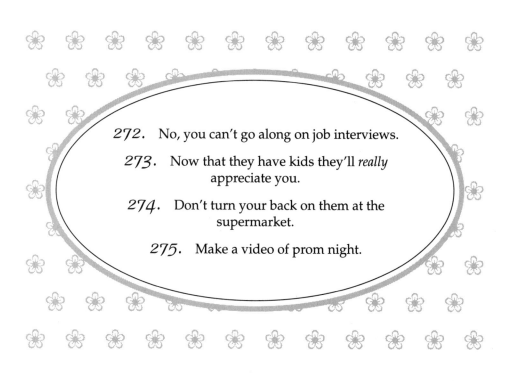

272. No, you can't go along on job interviews.

273. Now that they have kids they'll *really* appreciate you.

274. Don't turn your back on them at the supermarket.

275. Make a video of prom night.

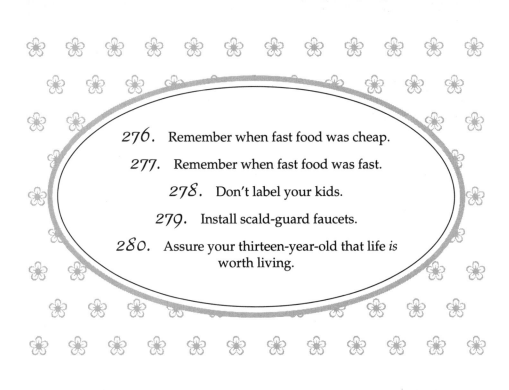

276. Remember when fast food was cheap.

277. Remember when fast food was fast.

278. Don't label your kids.

279. Install scald-guard faucets.

280. Assure your thirteen-year-old that life *is* worth living.

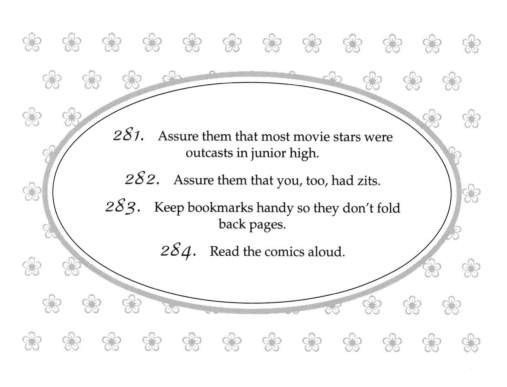

281. Assure them that most movie stars were outcasts in junior high.

282. Assure them that you, too, had zits.

283. Keep bookmarks handy so they don't fold back pages.

284. Read the comics aloud.

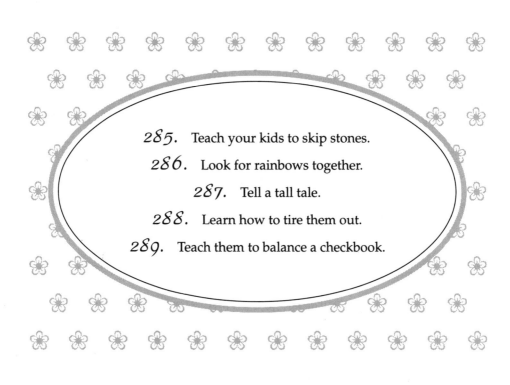

285. Teach your kids to skip stones.

286. Look for rainbows together.

287. Tell a tall tale.

288. Learn how to tire them out.

289. Teach them to balance a checkbook.

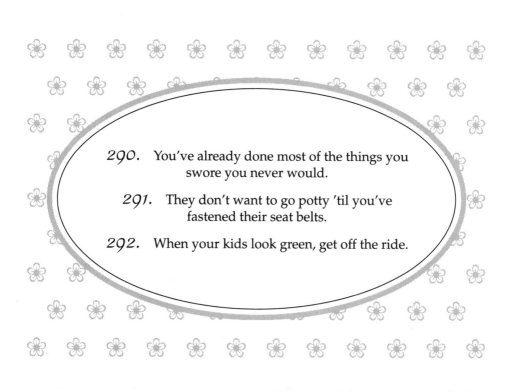

290. You've already done most of the things you swore you never would.

291. They don't want to go potty 'til you've fastened their seat belts.

292. When your kids look green, get off the ride.

293. One day, your two-year-old will point the remote control at you and try to turn you off.

294. Even when they're twenty, you like to sneak in at night and check their breathing.

295. Cheerios travel well.

296. Peeled bananas don't travel well.

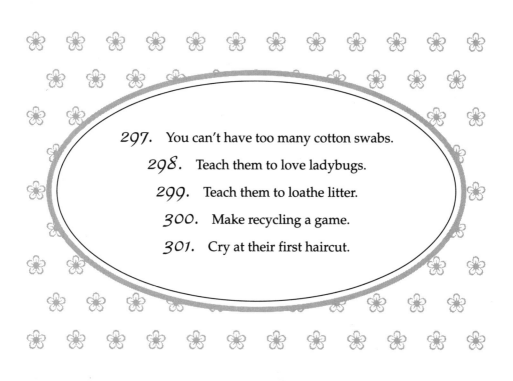

297. You can't have too many cotton swabs.

298. Teach them to love ladybugs.

299. Teach them to loathe litter.

300. Make recycling a game.

301. Cry at their first haircut.

302. Make a collage.

303. Let them make tree ornaments.

304. *The Flintstones* was better as a cartoon.

305. Say with feeling: *"You'll put your eye out."*

306. Set limits.

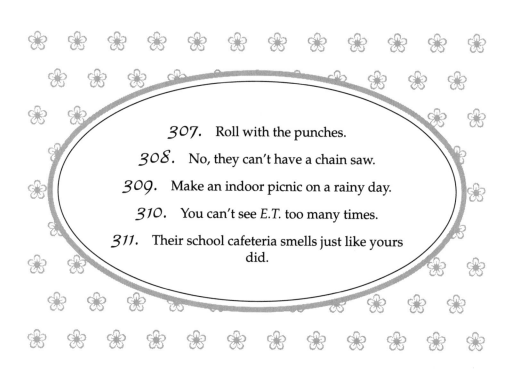

307. Roll with the punches.

308. No, they can't have a chain saw.

309. Make an indoor picnic on a rainy day.

310. You can't see *E.T.* too many times.

311. Their school cafeteria smells just like yours did.

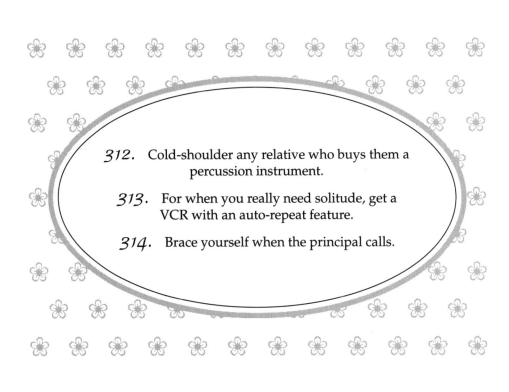

312. Cold-shoulder any relative who buys them a percussion instrument.

313. For when you really need solitude, get a VCR with an auto-repeat feature.

314. Brace yourself when the principal calls.

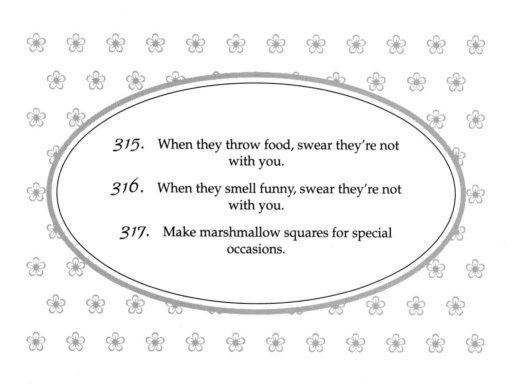

315. When they throw food, swear they're not with you.

316. When they smell funny, swear they're not with you.

317. Make marshmallow squares for special occasions.

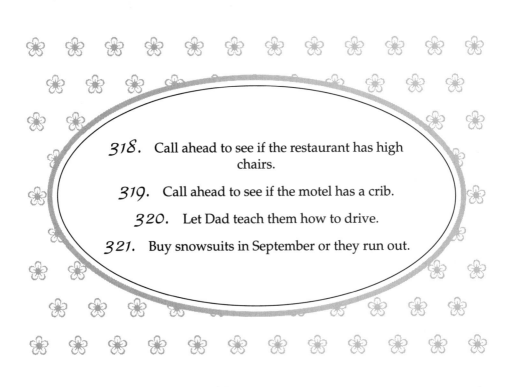

318. Call ahead to see if the restaurant has high chairs.

319. Call ahead to see if the motel has a crib.

320. Let Dad teach them how to drive.

321. Buy snowsuits in September or they run out.

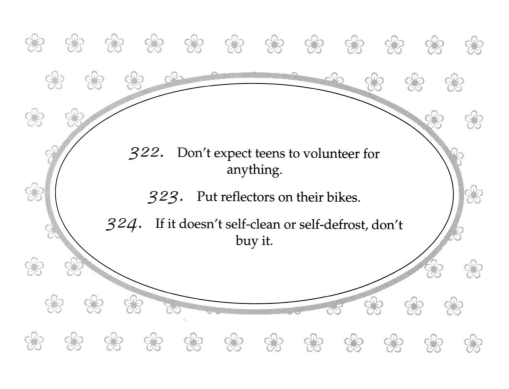

322. Don't expect teens to volunteer for anything.

323. Put reflectors on their bikes.

324. If it doesn't self-clean or self-defrost, don't buy it.

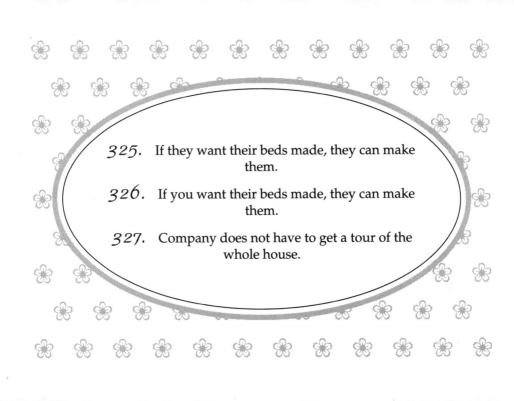

325. If they want their beds made, they can make
them.

326. If you want their beds made, they can make
them.

327. Company does not have to get a tour of the
whole house.

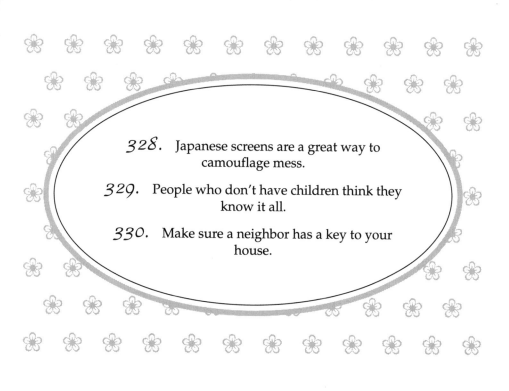

328. Japanese screens are a great way to camouflage mess.

329. People who don't have children think they know it all.

330. Make sure a neighbor has a key to your house.

331. A second bathroom is well worth the money.

332. Let them put the toll in the toll machine.

333. Keep an airsick bag in the car.

334. Keep napkins in the glove compartment.

335. Dual airbags, please.

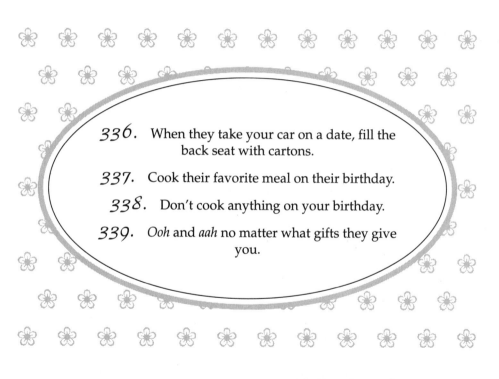

336. When they take your car on a date, fill the back seat with cartons.

337. Cook their favorite meal on their birthday.

338. Don't cook anything on your birthday.

339. *Ooh* and *aah* no matter what gifts they give you.

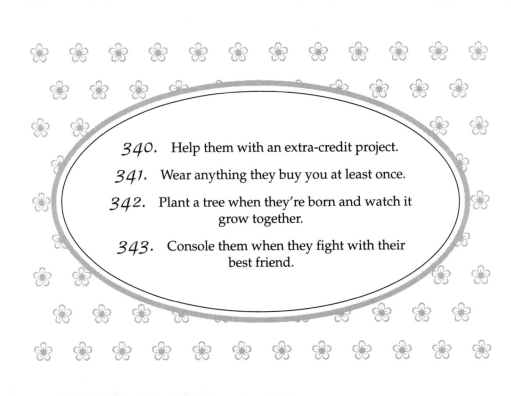

340. Help them with an extra-credit project.

341. Wear anything they buy you at least once.

342. Plant a tree when they're born and watch it grow together.

343. Console them when they fight with their best friend.

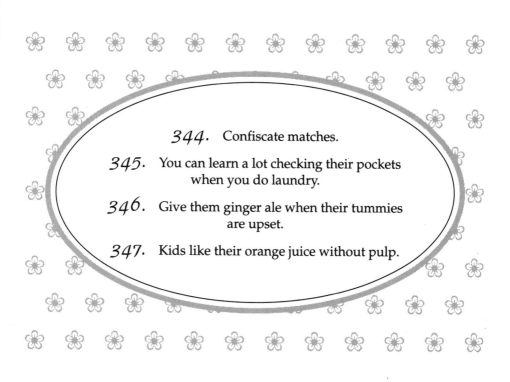

344. Confiscate matches.

345. You can learn a lot checking their pockets when you do laundry.

346. Give them ginger ale when their tummies are upset.

347. Kids like their orange juice without pulp.

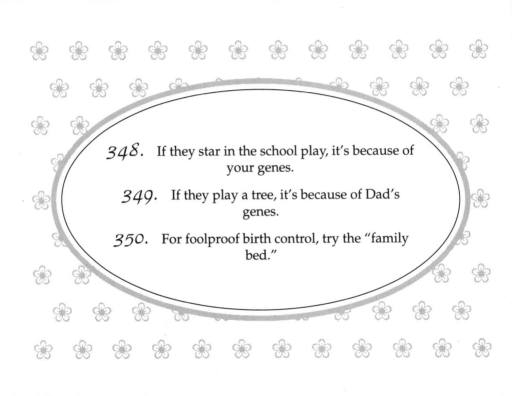

348. If they star in the school play, it's because of your genes.

349. If they play a tree, it's because of Dad's genes.

350. For foolproof birth control, try the "family bed."

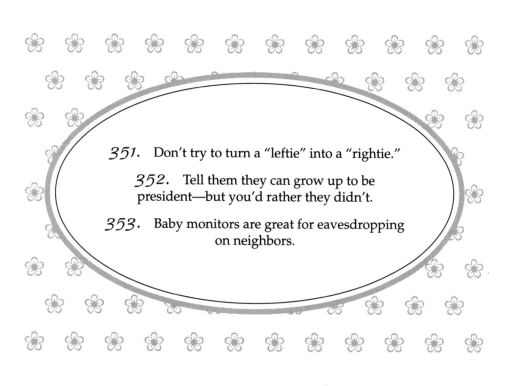

351. Don't try to turn a "leftie" into a "rightie."

352. Tell them they can grow up to be president—but you'd rather they didn't.

353. Baby monitors are great for eavesdropping on neighbors.

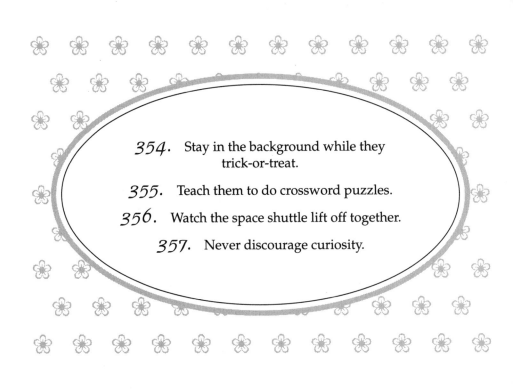

354. Stay in the background while they trick-or-treat.

355. Teach them to do crossword puzzles.

356. Watch the space shuttle lift off together.

357. Never discourage curiosity.

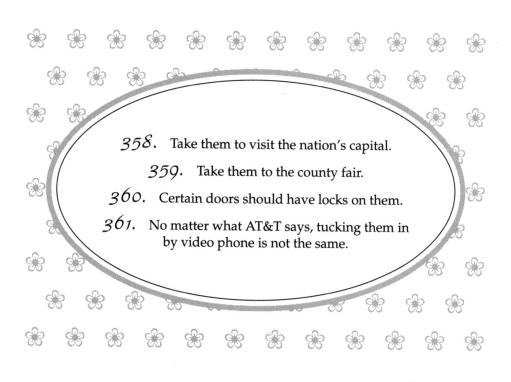

358. Take them to visit the nation's capital.

359. Take them to the county fair.

360. Certain doors should have locks on them.

361. No matter what AT&T says, tucking them in by video phone is not the same.

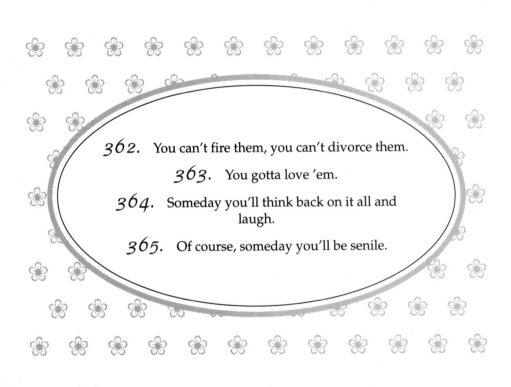

362. You can't fire them, you can't divorce them.

363. You gotta love 'em.

364. Someday you'll think back on it all and laugh.

365. Of course, someday you'll be senile.